FOREWORD

This guidebook was written by a team of members of the Ayrshire Archaeological and Natural History Society and Kyle and Carrick Civic Society: Sheila Allan, Rob Close, Sally Dickie, Merry Graham, Rob Graham, Trevor Mathews, Sheila Penny and Stanley Sarsfield. All the illustrations were specially drawn by John Doig.

The team consulted widely and is indebted to the many historians, farmers ministers, public officers and many others who made valuable contributions.

The printing was financed by an interest-free loan from the Prestwick Common Good Fund controlled by South Ayrshire Council.

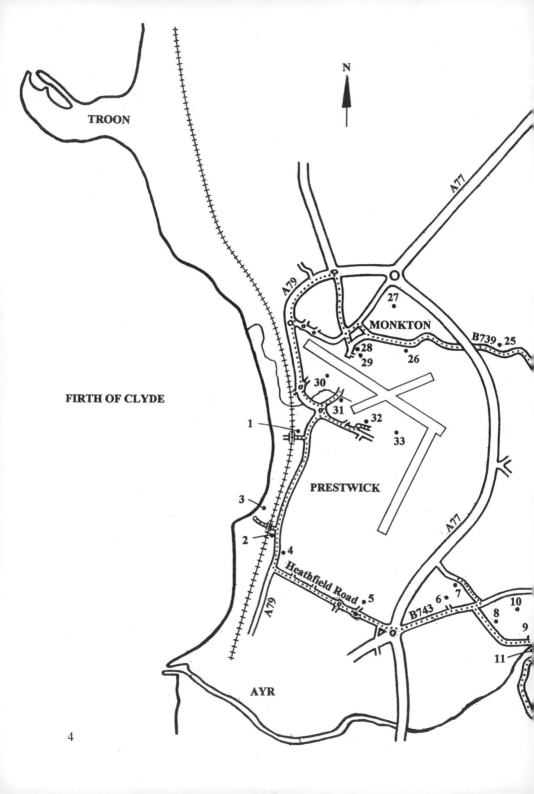

TROON

N

A77

A79

27

MONKTON

B739 • 25

28
29   • 26

FIRTH OF CLYDE

30
31
• 32

1

33

PRESTWICK

3

A77

2

4

Heathfield Road
• 5

A79

6 • 7

B743 • 6 • 7

10

• 8

9

11

AYR

4

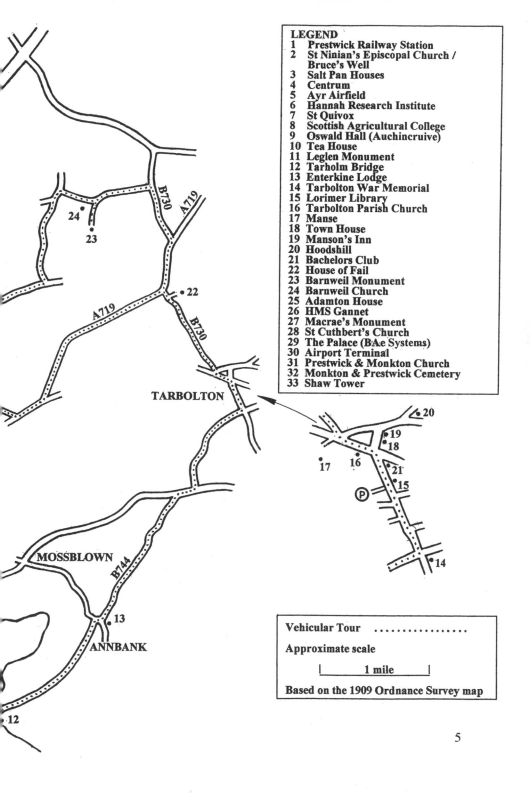

LEGEND
1. Prestwick Railway Station
2. St Ninian's Episcopal Church / Bruce's Well
3. Salt Pan Houses
4. Centrum
5. Ayr Airfield
6. Hannah Research Institute
7. St Quivox
8. Scottish Agricultural College
9. Oswald Hall (Auchincruive)
10. Tea House
11. Leglen Monument
12. Tarholm Bridge
13. Enterkine Lodge
14. Tarbolton War Memorial
15. Lorimer Library
16. Tarbolton Parish Church
17. Manse
18. Town House
19. Manson's Inn
20. Hoodshill
21. Bachelors Club
22. House of Fail
23. Barnweil Monument
24. Barnweil Church
25. Adamton House
26. HMS Gannet
27. Macrae's Monument
28. St Cuthbert's Church
29. The Palace (BAe Systems)
30. Airport Terminal
31. Prestwick & Monkton Church
32. Monkton & Prestwick Cemetery
33. Shaw Tower

Vehicular Tour . . . .

Approximate scale

|_____ 1 mile _____|

Based on the 1909 Ordnance Survey map

5

PRESTWICK

'Prestwick' conjures up several images. Some people will associate it with early golfers such as Tom Morris and the history of the Open Championship or see it as a holiday resort. Others will think of a thriving airport with a rich history.

The name Prestwick is first recorded in 1158, and means 'priest's dwelling' or 'priest's farm'. The name must have been in use for some hundreds of years before then, and mankind has occupied this area for much longer. Worked flints from the Stone Age, about 5000 BC, have been found at many sites in the area. In 750 AD Edbert of Northumbria annexed the plain of Kyle to his kingdom, and it seems plausible that Northumbrian monks arrived about this time, bringing both the Anglo-Saxon or Old English language, and veneration for St Cuthbert (who died in 687), to whom the church at Monkton is dedicated.

Prestwick was created a burgh in the 12th century. However it did not grow in the way that the neighbouring town of Ayr did, and remained, until the early 19th century, a small community: a village with some of the trappings of a burgh, concerned largely with farming, and with associated home industries such as weaving. Salt was manufactured at the coast.

Change, slow at first, began in 1840 when the Glasgow to Ayr railway opened. The trains brought golfers, summer visitors and, in due course, commuters, and the Prestwick we know today began to take shape. Coal mining has come and gone. An international airport and the manufacture of aircraft components are major sources of employment.

We shall learn more of the town, its history and its personalities in a group of walks in the first part of this guide. The second part, from page 27, will help you to explore the surrounding countryside and villages by car or bicycle.

Our aim has been a balanced presentation of the archaeology, history, buildings, scenery and personalities that have made Prestwick and its surroundings what it is today, so that each reader will find those features which particularly interest him or her placed in their historic, economic and social context.

The walks include a few extensions, each of which opens with a row of three arrows and usually a heading. If you do not wish to include the extension in your walk, go to where it is closed by another three arrows, where you will find the main route continuing.

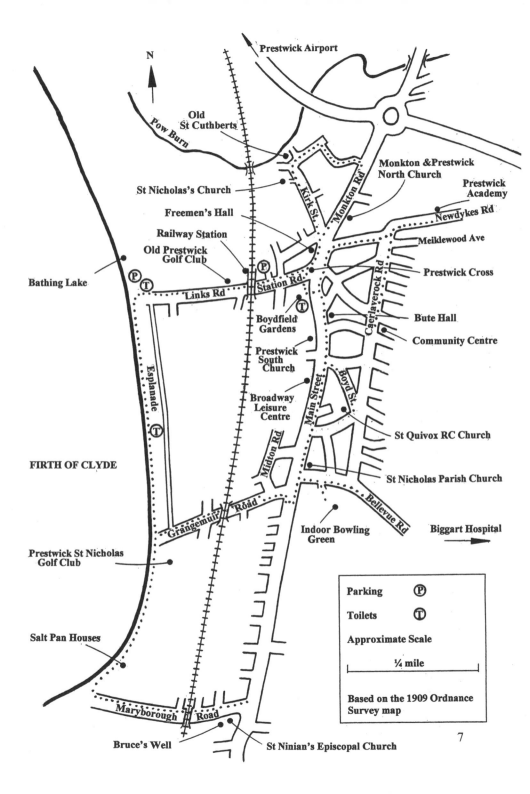

N

Prestwick Airport

Pow Burn

Old St Cuthberts

St Nicholas's Church

Freemen's Hall

Railway Station

Old Prestwick Golf Club

Bathing Lake

Kirk St.

Monkton Rd

Monkton &Prestwick North Church

Prestwick Academy

Newdykes Rd

Meiklewood Ave

Prestwick Cross

Caerlaverock Rd

Bute Hall

Community Centre

Links Rd

Station Rd

Boydfield Gardens

Prestwick South Church

Broadway Leisure Centre

Esplanade

FIRTH OF CLYDE

Main Street

Boyd St.

St Quivox RC Church

St Nicholas Parish Church

Midton Rd

Grangemuir Road

Bellevue Rd

Biggart Hospital

Indoor Bowling Green

Prestwick St Nicholas Golf Club

Salt Pan Houses

Maryborough Road

Bruce's Well

St Ninian's Episcopal Church

| Parking | Ⓟ |
| Toilets | Ⓣ |

Approximate Scale

¼ mile

Based on the 1909 Ordnance Survey map

7

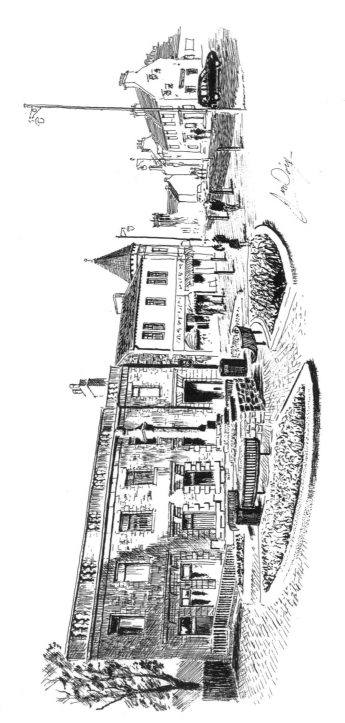

Prestwick's Mercat Cross

Prestwick Mercat Cross walk, 1½ miles, taking in the Cross, Freemen's Hall and the medieval church of St Nicholas

The walk begins at **Prestwick Town railway station**. The present station buildings date from about 1900; the main block is a pleasant harled single-storey block with red sandstone details. There is a public car park here, alongside the station car park, and additional parking is available at the sea-front at the foot of Links Road. From the car park, enter the station and climb the footbridge. From here the taller visitor gains a good impression of Prestwick and its surrounding area. Looking north along the railway line, to your left is Prestwick Golf Club, with its prominent clubhouse close to the railway, and the links stretching towards the sea. Beyond are the shore, the Firth of Clyde and its islands; there is a good view of Arran, and Lady Isle sits low in the water. Although much tamed, the 'rough' of the golf links - sandy hillocks and whin bushes - gives a good impression of how all this area must once have appeared. Ahead, to the right of the railway, are Prestwick's ivy-clad medieval church and, beyond, the substantial buildings of the airport. To your right is the commercial heart of the town, with the spire of the Freemen's Hall. Behind you the railway cuts through the residential heartland of Prestwick. Landmarks in this direction include the grey spire of Prestwick South Church and the red sandstone tower of St Nicholas Church. The view is closed by the Carrick Hills, south of Ayr.

Prestwick Golf Club from station footbridge

Walk out through the car park, and turn left into Station Road, crossing Station Drive and Mansewell Road (which is only a footpath at this point). On the opposite side of Station Road, at the entrance to the public park, originally

9

known as the Well Green, is a lamp-post on a granite base, with a bronze portrait medallion by Robert Bryden. This dates from 1904 and was a gift to the town from Matthew Smith (1832-1908), a member of the Town Council. He was one of a number of wealthy merchants and professional men from Kilmarnock who moved to Prestwick during its rapid expansion around 1900. His gift was erected at Prestwick Cross, where it served as a drinking fountain and horse-trough. It was severely truncated and moved to its present position in 1913.

Continuing along Station Road, you come on the left to a stately pair of late 19th-century houses known as Haddington Park. The first of these, with the wrought iron porch, was the home of Glasgow architect John Keppie (1862-1945) of Honeyman and Keppie, who was one of the first to recognise the talent of, and employ, Charles Rennie Mackintosh.

> Mackintosh visited the Keppie home in Prestwick, sometimes with Herbert McNair, who together with John Keppie would work here on drawings for competitions. They would be joined by Jessie Keppie, the youngest sister, herself a student of Glasgow School of Art, and other members of the group who called themselves 'The Immortals', including Frances and Margaret MacDonald. Between 1892 and 1894 Mackintosh was reputedly engaged to Jessie Keppie, and it was for her that he made the *repoussé* brass casket which is now in the Victoria and Albert Museum, London. At the 1933 Memorial Exhibition of Mackintosh's work, Jessie bought his watercolour painting 'White Roses', which on her death in 1951 she bequeathed to Glasgow School of Art. Jessie Keppie, her brother John and two of their sisters are buried in Prestwick cemetery.

Continuing, you quickly arrive at **Prestwick Cross**. The Cross itself is a simple hexagonal shaft with a pedimented top and ball finial. It has the inscription 'Prestick' and 'Rebuilt 1777'. The Cross has stood in several places in its time, being moved because it was in the way of traffic. In the 19th century the Cross was the centre of village life. To the left of the Cross is the Post Office, a confident classical design from 1927. Continue walking past the Post Office, and the row of shops running from there to the Freemen's Hall. The last of these shops, now used as an office by South Ayrshire Council, was the first clubhouse of Prestwick Merchants' Golf Club, which became St Nicholas Golf Club, and alongside was that of Prestwick Golf Club, about 1851, in which Tom Morris lived and sold golf balls, and where the members stored their equipment.

Next to the Council office is the **Freemen's Hall**. This was built in 1844 as a meeting place for the thirty-six Freemen of Prestwick, who had power and

10

responsibility in many areas of village life. They owned the farmland, were responsible for its distribution and management, and also had the power to hold civil and criminal courts. This Freemen's Hall also contained a schoolroom. In 1903 it became the meeting place for Prestwick Burgh Council, which was established that year. The Hall has a Gothic spire, and a clock set in a decorative strapwork panel.

The Freemen's Hall

The 36 Prestwick Freemen held the lands of Prestwick communally. For much of the medieval period they were in effect the managers of the town. Similarly, 48 Freemen managed neighbouring Newton on Ayr. The communal ownership of land, and the regular redistribution of the lots or dales, into which the pasture land and arable land was divided, hindered agricultural and industrial development in the 18th and early 19th centuries. The Freemen, however, were able to sell land to the railway company and built the Freemen's Hall from the proceeds. In 1833 the holdings at that time were converted into long leases, and the removal of legal restrictions in 1850 enabled the individual freemen to sell the land. That marked the birth of modern

11

Prestwick. In the 20th century Prestwick Town Council, which had assumed most of the functions of the Freemen, granted Honorary Freedoms to David F. McIntyre and the Duke of Hamilton, the founders of Prestwick Airport (see p.47 and p.56); to Thomas McClure (Provost from 1912 to 1916), and to Matthew Foulds, who was involved with Scouting in Prestwick for over 50 years.

Almost all signs of coal mining have vanished, but there were coal workings in the burgh in the 16th century and at Prestwick Toll in the early 19th century. In 1903, however, the Freemen of Prestwick leased the coal under the burgh to the Auchincruive Coal Company. A pit was sunk at Glenburn, east of Prestwick, and production began in 1912. The company built a substantial village of colliers' houses. In 1964 a thousand men were employed at Glenburn. Production ceased in 1973. The former office block of the National Coal Board (which took over most collieries in 1947) is now known as Atlantic House, and is part of Britain's Air Traffic Control service.

Turn left at the Freemen's Hall into **Kirk Street**. It was one of the original streets of the village, where almost every house was a weaver's shop. It has been redeveloped over the years, and only a few much-altered single-storey cottages survive to give any impression of how it may once have looked. With a loom catching light from the window, and storage space taken up by yarn and finished work, these dwellings must have been very crowded.

Continue along Kirk Street. Immediately after number 37 there is a wide grassy path leading up to the entrance to **St Nicholas Church and kirkyard**.

St Nicholas Church and Kirkyard

This venerable structure stands on a mound surrounded by an old burial ground. The site is clearly one of some antiquity, and may have been used for Christian worship since the Northumbrian monks arrived here in the 8th century. What we see today is later, and may represent, in part, the church granted to Paisley Abbey by Walter Fitzalan around 1170, and mentioned in a Charter of Paisley Abbey dated 1212. It is a simple oblong and very plain: it has buttresses at the east end, an equally simple belfry and an earthen floor. It must have been altered after the Reformation, when the square-headed windows would have been inserted. Hewat (see p.15) says that a gallery ran the length of one wall to within touching distance of the pulpit, while the men of the congregation worshipped in a loft reached by an open wooden ladder. From 1571 a single minister served Prestwick and Monkton: from this time, or shortly thereafter, for a large number of years, the custom was to have services on two successive Sundays in Monkton, followed by one Sunday in Prestwick. The amalgamation of the parishes, and the bias towards Monkton in the distribution of services, is indicative of how little the burgh and village of Prestwick had grown; more so, when it is remembered that until 1779 the town of Newton on Ayr had been part of Prestwick parish.

In the kirkyard there are a number of interesting carved stones, some showing the tools of the deceased's trade. One particularly attractive example, close to the path and facing you as you approach the church, shows cogged wheels, millstones and a miller's shovel. Look out for the traditional symbols of mortality, such as the skull, cross-bones and winged hourglass. South of the church, near the boundary, is a grave slab held down by iron bars, a precaution against 'resurrection men' (body snatchers). A church on a prominent knowe such as this often indicates an early religious site. The ground was closed for new burials in 1906.

Tradition says that there are graves of Knights Templar and a Covenanter here. However, there are no stones that can definitely be linked to any of these. Even by the end of the 19th century the supposed Covenanter's stone could not be pointed out, and his name had been forgotten.

Return by the grassy path and turn left along Kirk Street. At its end, where the road curves to the left, is Seagate (the way to the sea). This becomes a footpath going under the railway and crossing the golf course. It leads towards the mouth of the **Pow Burn**. This short but vigorous stream marks the boundary between Prestwick and Monkton. It used to be highly regarded as a good spot for line-fishing of salmon. When the easiest route for pedestrians and horsemen between Ayr and Irvine was along the shore, the mouth of the Pow Burn provided the major obstacles: a fast-flowing stream to ford, and shifting quicksands to avoid. The Armstrongs' map of Ayrshire in 1775 bears the legend 'There is a dangerous quick Sand on the Road at the Foot of Pow burn to avoid it keep as near the Sea as the Tide will allow.'

> The early part of the sixteenth century was marked in Ayrshire by a number of vicious feuds between several of the county's powerful families. One long-running dispute was between the Kennedys, especially the Kennedys of Cassillis and Bargany, from the south of the county, and the Campbells and Craufurds, from the centre and north. In 1527 Gilbert Kennedy, Earl of Cassillis, was ambushed and killed near the Pow Burn by a group of Campbells and Crawfords. Although not present, Hugh Campbell of Loudoun, the Sheriff of Ayrshire, had connived at the murder. Others implicated in the crime included George Craufurd of Leifnorris, John Craufurd of Drongan and John Campbell of Cessnock.

At the junction with McIntyre Road, turn right, following the cycle route signs. At this junction, amongst more recent housing, is a charming Arts-and-Crafts structure, now called Old St Cuthberts. Built in 1908, this was the clubhouse of **Prestwick St Cuthberts Golf Club**. This club was formed, and links here opened, in 1899, but in 1960 the course was lost to airport and road developments, and the golfers moved to a new site in East Road, Prestwick. Their old clubhouse became a club for employees at the airport, but has now been converted, and extended, for residential use. Walk down Macrae Drive and look back for a good view of the original elevation.

Further along McIntyre Road, the striking modern building behind the houses on the left is a sewage pumping station.

Sewage pumping station

Still following the cycle route signs, turn right into the paved Capper View, named after Noel Capper, chief test pilot of Scottish Aviation Ltd. At the end a broad path leads to Monkton Road. When you reach it, look left to see the pinnacled tower of the former Monkton and Prestwick Parish Church (see p.46 and p.49), built half-way between the two settlements. Then walk right along Monkton Road. There are a number of good late Victorian houses opposite, especially numbers 44 and 46, with their stonework in contrasting colours. You now pass, on the right, The Crescent, 29-43 Monkton Road, a neat development of 1901-1902, with similar houses on the other side of Monkton Road. Further along, on the left, is Monkton and Prestwick North Parish Church, with its former manse to the left.

Monkton and Prestwick North Parish Church was the Free Church of Prestwick, built in 1874, and enlarged in 1896. From 1900 to 1929 it was known as Prestwick North U.F. Church. Halls to the left and rear were added in 1932. In 1987, the congregation was merged with that of Prestwick St Cuthberts, this church becoming the church of the amalgamated congregation. The original church is a simple rectangle of stone from the Bellrock quarry at Prestwick Toll. The 60-foot-high bell tower dominating the facade was added in 1895-96, incorporating the sculpted 'Burning Bush', which had been in the gable of the original church. The architect of the tower was John Kcppie (see p.10). Two stained glass windows were installed in 1910. One commemorates the mother and mother-in-law of Kirkwood Hewat, and the other commemorates the Rev Dr Thomas Burns (see p.46 and p.50).

> Kirkwood Hewat (1856-1927) was the best-known minister of Prestwick North Church, which he served from 1881 until 1915. He wrote a history of Prestwick, *A Little Scottish World,* published in 1894. He was born in Edinburgh, where his father was a banker, and educated there and in Leipzig. Hewat had wide-ranging interests, and his books and articles span not only local history, but also many subjects from church history to foreign travel. He lived in the Manse, built in 1885, which adjoins the church to its left.

Further along on the left can be seen the traditional frontage of the **Eagle Tavern**, and also that of the **Red Lion**. As explained by a notice on the wall, the Golf Club of Ayrshire (the forerunner of Prestwick Golf Club) was founded at a meeting in the Red Lion in 1851 (see p.26).

You are now back at Prestwick Cross. Use one set of pedestrian-controlled lights to cross Station Road to the **War Memorial** (1921). It is a complex symbolic design by James Λ. Morris, carved from stone from Woodburn Quarry, Northumberland, with bronzes by the Glasgow sculptor James A Young.

War Memorial and former Town Hall

Behind the War Memorial is a public park, **Boydfield Gardens**, on the site of Boydfield House, which was demolished in 1933. There were ambitious plans for a new Civic Centre to be built here, but the Second World War put an end to this scheme, leaving this open space at the heart of the town. In the middle of the garden there are two sundials. The smaller, in a traditional pattern, was erected in 1959 to celebrate the 50th anniversary of the Boy Scout troop in Prestwick. The larger, with many attractive and naturalistic designs in blue-painted steel and cast iron, was unveiled in June 1998. It is the work of pupils at Prestwick Academy, assisted by the Balfron artist Elspeth Bennie.

After pausing to look at the former Town Hall building opposite, use the pedestrian-controlled lights to cross Main Street to the Clydesdale Bank.

►►►
Extension to Prestwick Academy, 1 mile

It is possible to make a digression here. Turn left on reaching the Clydesdale Bank, and re-pass the Red Lion and the Eagle, reaching Alexandra Avenue, formerly known as The Vennel. Turn down Alexandra Avenue, passing Kirkhall Surgery, formerly a church hall, and at the end turn left into Caerlaverock Road, and then follow Newdykes Road round to the right. At the junction is Powbank, 1 Newdykes Road, formerly a farm.

> Along Newdykes Road, **Prestwick Academy** is on your left. It opened in 1902 with 122 pupils enrolled, of whom 82 paid fees ranging from three to eight shillings a quarter. It was renamed Prestwick Academy in 1968, and it is now able to cope with a roll of between 900 and 1000. The gate piers are enlivened by steel sculptures - a further result of the collaboration between Academy pupils and Elspeth Bennie.

Return to the junction of Alexandra Avenue and Caerlaverock Road, and continue along Caerlaverock Road until you come to the **former Prestwick Public School**, which opened in 1882. Until it was built, classes were held in the Freemen's Hall. It became the Community Centre in 1971, when Kingcase Primary School opened. Return to the Cross by Caerlaverock Road and Alexandra Avenue.

> In the small public open space at the junction of Alexandra Avenue and Caerlaverock Road are four ivy-covered concrete blocks. These are part of an anti-tank defence system erected in Prestwick during the Second World War. Throughout the burgh there are metal plates in the road, with the name of the Ayr founders A & J Hunter on them. These cover the sockets which were the anchors for further anti-tank obstacles composed of steel beams. Examples of these anchorage points can be seen in Meiklewood Avenue nearby, six outside Number 3 and six outside Number 4. There are others in Main Street. Where possible, the steelwork for the new blocks was stored clear of the roadway to give free passage, especially during the blackout.

◄◄◄

Main Street southwards to St Nicholas Church, returning by the shore, 1½ miles. Covers the commercial and recreational centre of Prestwick, and its seafront

Having crossed to the Clydesdale Bank, turn right to walk along Main Street. This tall red sandstone building, with shops on the ground floor, and upper floors distinguished by tall 2-storey windows, was originally the Prestwick Unionist Club. It was built in 1899 and subsequently became Prestwick Town

Hall. From 1919 until 1922 it was owned by the Prestwick Cinema Company. It was then sold to the Town Council and used as municipal offices. It was later converted into flats.

Continue along Main Street. The **Police Station** across the road occupies two buildings. The older one was built in 1903. On this side we cross Sauterne Road (a clue to the meaning of this unusual name may be in the returns of the Census for 1881 where it is given as 'Sauntering Road'), and then pass the Bute Hall, a hall of the Christian Brethren since it was built about 1890. It was substantially rebuilt in 1954. Nearby is the **65 Club.** It occupies two houses which had formerly been the offices of Monkton and Prestwick Parochial Board, where poor relief was administered and distributed. In the early 1960s they were acquired by Prestwick Town Council from the County Council and converted into a social centre and clubrooms: '65' is the house number, but it also tells us that the club welcomes all senior citizens.

A little further along on the opposite side is **Prestwick South Church**. This was Prestwick's United Presbyterian church, and was opened in 1884. It is built of grey freestone from Craiksland Quarry near Loans. The original church, the hall at the rear, was built in 1879-1880, but replaced almost immediately. Although clearly built to a tight budget, the South Church has some attractive Arts-and-Crafts details, as befits a building designed by the renowned Ayr architect, James A Morris. It also has an excellent War Memorial stained glass window by Oscar Paterson, and a noteworthy Millennium window, installed in 2000.

Continuing along Main Street, both sides display an interesting mix of small locally owned shops, bars and cafés. The presence of these businesses and the relative scarcity of national chains help give Prestwick its character. Just past the Central Bar, Kyle Street runs off Main Street. **Prestwick Library**, in Kyle Street, opened in 1947. It was originally a billiards hall built in 1925. On our side of Main Street, we now cross Gardiner Street. Boyd Street, formerly known as Smiddy Row, branches right about 50 yards along Gardiner Street.

> Robert Brown (about 1829-1916) generally regarded as the last of the hand-loom weavers in Prestwick, lived and worked at 2 Boyd Street (now demolished) until his death. As well as weaving silk handkerchiefs himself, he acted as an agent, negotiating between the weavers and the cloth manufacturers in Glasgow and elsewhere. Displaced by power-loom factories, hand-loom weavers had to adapt and specialise to survive: Prestwick's forté became silk handkerchiefs. A flag celebrating the relief of Mafeking was also produced. This is now in private hands in Prestwick.

Another well-known resident of Smiddy Row was John Gray (1824-1904) who lived and worked at the Smithy. Although he was a blacksmith, he is best remembered as one of the first master makers of golf clubs - or 'cleeks' as they were known in the 19th Century. Clubs manufactured by Gray are now much sought after by collectors of golf memorabilia.

If you follow Boyd Street to its junction with Caerlaverock Road and St Quivox Road, you will find Prestwick's Roman Catholic Church: St Quivox. This is an imposing and uncompromising design from 1932-33: a big block of red brick with few windows and one stained glass window on the south side. A new church hall was built adjacent to the church in 2001. Return via Boyd Street to the main route.

Continuing along Main Street, look at numbers 72-74 on the opposite side. At first floor level there is one surviving cast iron rosette. Fixings of this type held the overhead wires for the Ayr Corporation trams which ran between Prestwick Cross and the Burns Monument at Alloway from 1901 until 1931. Also on this side is the **Broadway**, an exercise in bright white cubes, and originally the Broadway Cinema. It opened in April 1935 and closed in 1965, though it re-opened for a few months in 1976. The architect was Alister G. Macdonald, the son of Prime Minister Ramsay Macdonald. The first film shown was *The Barretts of Wimpole Street*, starring Charles Laughton and Frederic March.

The Broadway

Midton, the elegant grey sandstone house at 94 Main Street, was long the home of Charles Hunter (1836-1921), who had a long association with Prestwick Golf Club.

> Hunter worked in a lawyer's office in Ayr, and later with the Customs and Excise service, but golf was his passion. He took part in the first Open, the Competition for the Belt in 1860, and so became, almost by default, a professional golfer. He was trained by the elder Tom Morris to become a skilled maker of balls and clubs. He succeeded Morris as the professional at Prestwick in 1864, but left the following year for a similar position at Blackheath, London. When his successor, Andrew Strath, died in 1868, Hunter was invited back to Prestwick and remained with the club, in various capacities, until his death 53 years later. Hunter became the Grand Old Man of golf in the west of Scotland.

As we pass along the next stretch of Main Street, we can again recognise the mixture of long-established local shops and cafés that distinguish Prestwick. Among the bars, the **Caprice** occupies the stylish 1950s building (114-116 Main Street) that was originally the British Linen Bank.

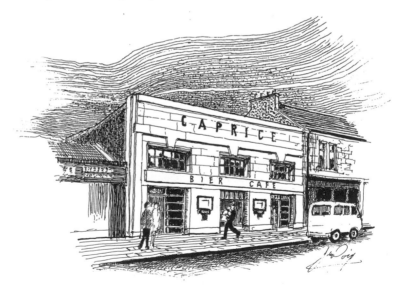

Caprice

Continuing, **St Nicholas Parish Church**, set back from the road, is seen on the left. This church was built in 1907-08, to accommodate the growing population at this end of Prestwick. It was designed by the Glasgow architect-conservationist Peter MacGregor Chalmers, and is very similar to his church at Kinneil, Bo'ness. The style he has adopted is a very mannered approach to Norman architecture. It is built of Ballochmyle stone, and the assured west tower is a prominent landmark in an area where bungalows predominate. The glory of the church is its splendid collection of stained glass windows, many of them the work of the Abbey Studio in Glasgow. A new stained glass window was installed in 2002, designed and made by Moira Parker and entitled 'The Light of the World'.

St Nicholas Manse is to the right of the church, in Bellevue Road.

Opposite there is a small public car-park, adjoining St Ninian's Park (also known as the Oval), which was opened in 1954 on land which had previously been a municipal golf course - Ladies St Nicholas Golf Links. This had opened in 1936 and closed in 1953, when part of the land was lost to housing development. The park is now home to several leisure facilities.

St Nicholas Parish Church

Close by is the ground of **Prestwick Cricket Club**. This club had formerly been Ayr Craigie, becoming Prestwick Cricket Club, and moving here in 1954. It is now one of the leading club sides in Scotland. Beyond the cricket pitch is a large new **indoor tennis court complex**.

The **Indoor Bowling Green** was opened in 1964, the second to be built in Scotland. It has murals rescued from the old airport terminal building at Orangefield. These are by Tom Gilfillan and portray important cities. It is open 10 a.m. to 4 p.m. Monday to Friday. Visitors are welcome, particularly in the afternoons, during May, June and July. The **Indoor Swimming Pool** opened in 1975, and in 2001 The **Space Place**, Prestwick's youth centre opened. This has a large café-lounge, and audio and IT equipment.

Return to St Nicholas Church.

► ► ►
Extension to Biggart Hospital, 3/4 mile

It is also possible to continue along Bellevue Road, crossing Adamton Road, and entering Biggart Road.

On the left is the **Biggart Hospital**. This opened in 1905 as the Biggart Memorial Home for Cripple Children. It was run by the Glasgow United Evangelistic Association, through their Fresh Air Fortnight Scheme, which gave inhabitants of the smoky cities and towns of west central Scotland holidays in purer air. The scheme had been established in 1884, and when the Biggart was opened the Association had eleven Homes and Weary Workers' Rests in the west of Scotland.

> The Biggart was founded by the children of Robert and Mary Biggart of Drumbuie, Beith, as a memorial to their parents, and to mark their mother's interest in the welfare of crippled children. In 1945 Ayrshire County Council Education Committee took over responsibility for the Biggart. At that time it was used as residential accommodation for convalescent children from Glasgow and Ayrshire. There were about 100 children in 1949, but by 1961 this was reduced to 69. In 1966 it was transferred to the Hospital Board (eventually Ayrshire and Arran Health Board). The Biggart has undergone many changes over the years and is now a very up-to-date geriatric hospital. The stained glass window from the original house was transferred to the Chapel of the new Ayr Hospital when it opened in 1991 [see *Historic Alloway*].

Biggart Hospital

Return to St Nicholas Church.
◄◄◄

Cross Bellevue Road and Main Street at the pedestrian controlled lights. Walk down Grangemuir Road.

►►►

Midton Road, on the right, offers an alternative return to the station: it emerges on to Station Road opposite the entrance to the car park. It is predominantly residential. Much of this road and the surrounding streets are built on an area known as The Bog, which was only properly drained early in the 20th century, and most of the houses here date from the early years of that century, and make a noteworthy contrast with the earlier developments which almost surround them. Although few call for detailed comment, the observant will find many interesting period details among these houses.
◄◄◄

Continue along Grangemuir Road and pass, with care, under the railway bridge. Shortly, on your left, you will see the links and clubhouse of **Prestwick St Nicholas Golf Club**. It was formed in 1851 as the Prestwick Merchants' Club and initially shared the links of Prestwick Golf Club. The new name was adopted in 1858. The new links were opened in 1892 and the clubhouse shortly afterwards. It has been much extended since but still to be seen on the far side of the clubhouse is a stone bas-relief of a golfer at play, the work of W.G. Stevenson, a noted Edinburgh sculptor whose other works include the Burns Statue in Chicago.

Just beyond the entrance to the golf club we meet the **Esplanade**. On our left are a health club and Prestwick Sailing Club. They are on the site of a pavilion built in 1910 by Prestwick Town Council for pierrot and minstrel shows. The pavilion was demolished in 1938. The attractive railings were erected about 1995.

Alternative route passing the Salt Pan Houses, 3/4 mile

The walking distance is the same as that of the last leg of the main route, but it leads to Ayr Road and buses back to Station Road

From here it is possible to turn left and walk along the Esplanade, as far as the Salt Pan Houses (see p.28). You could then continue from the Salt Pan Houses up Maryborough Road to its junction with Ayr Road and return to Prestwick Cross by any of the frequent buses travelling towards your left. This route passes the features described on pp.27-29.

Turn right along the Esplanade, laid out by the Burgh Council in 1908. It has sweeping views of the Firth of Clyde and its islands, including Ailsa Craig, to the left, and a varying progression of seaside villas to the right. None is especially outstanding, but all are well built, and are often planned to make full use of the magnificent views and sunsets. A quarter of a mile further on, about a hundred yards past the children's playground, you will see in the grounds of one of the villas a concrete eagle on a stone plinth. The villa is Stonegarth, the Royal Air Force Association Club. The eagle is a memorial to Polish sailors who lost their lives in the Battle of the Atlantic, 1939-1945. The memorial stood originally at Monkton Camp, which was on Prestwick Golf Course on the road towards the Prestwick Holiday Park. The house to the north (or left) of

24

Stonegarth is Ardayre, one of the first houses to be built west of the railway. It was built about 1867 for William Wilson (1823-1892), a Glasgow businessman.

Wilson was a noted philanthropist: the creation of a Burns Department at the Mitchell Library, Glasgow, was due to him. He also chaired the committee that oversaw the erection of the statue of Burns in George Square, Glasgow. In Prestwick he was a generous benefactor, especially to the Christian Brethren, and was a well-known figure on the golf links, dressed in the scarlet coat of the St Andrews Club.

A beach shelter with a verandah (1922) marks the junction of the Esplanade with Links Road.

▶▶▶

It is possible to walk further along the Esplanade, passing the site of the Prestwick Bathing Lake and a children's indoor play area followed by a modern sewage pumping station. This walk can be extended as far as the mouth of the Pow Burn (see p.13 and p.14).

Between 1931 and 1972 a very popular draw with both residents and visitors was the Open Air Bathing Lake. It could accommodate 1200 bathers and 3000 spectators. During the summer the Burgh Council provided galas, demonstrations by world-class swimmers and divers, fireworks, and moonlight bathing; but the most popular event was probably the annual Bathing Beauty competition, which regularly brought Prestwick national attention.

◀◀◀

Turn right into Links Road (there is no sign). The first house on the right is Greystone, built about 1898 for a Glasgow businessman, Robert Bryce. In the years before the First World War it was the home of Janie Allan, a prominent supporter of the women's suffrage movement in Scotland. Later the house was a nursing home for forty years before being divided.

Janie Allan was the daughter of Alexander Allan, owner of the Allan Shipping Line. The Allans were committed socialists. She helped to form the Glasgow and West of Scotland Association for Women's Suffrage in 1902, but joined the Women's Social and Political Union when it began to organise in Scotland in 1906. Her militancy began in 1911 in the North Ayrshire by-election, when she addressed several meetings. In 1912 she was sentenced to four months' imprisonment in Holloway for breaking windows. 10,500 Glaswegians signed a petition protesting about her imprisonment. When Emmeline Pankhurst was sent to Holloway jail the suffragette prisoners were ordered by the WSPU to hunger strike. Janie Allan barricaded herself in her cell and it took three men with crowbars to force the door open. She was forcibly fed for a week and later said that though originally in good health she took three months to recover.

On the left of Links Road are the links and club house of **Prestwick Golf Club**.

From about 1850 a number of gentlemen had paid an annual fee to the Freemen for the right to play golf along the links from the Saltpans at Maryborough to the Pow Burn. In 1850 one of them, James Ogilvie Fairlie of Coodham, persuaded 57 gentlemen from the west of Scotland to attend a meeting in the Red Lion, Prestwick, on 2nd July 1851, at which the Prestwick Golf Club was officially established. The club leased land between the railway and the shore, and appointed Tom Morris to lay out a 12-hole course, and to act as greenkeeper. The club flourished, and instituted the Open Championship (see below). A clubhouse was built in 1866: this has now been considerably extended and bears little resemblance to the original small villa. The club remains one of the most exclusive and prestigious in Scottish golf.

Close to Links Road is a small **cairn**. This was unveiled by Henry Cotton in 1977 and marks the first hole of the first Open Championship, held 17 October 1860. In 1860 the Prestwick Golf Club put up the money for a Championship Belt. Though it was open to any golfer this first Open Championship attracted only eight entrants. It was won by Willie Park from Musselburgh. The event, however, was deemed to be a success, and was repeated in successive years. Prestwick's Tom Morris won the Belt four times in the 1860s, and his son, Tom Morris junior, won for the third successive year in 1870 and secured permanent ownership of the Belt. In 1872 he was the first winner of the replacement Cup, which remains the trophy played for each year.

Thomas Morris Junior (1851-1875). 'Young Tom' Morris is regarded as one of the best golfers of all time: his record of four successive wins in the Open will probably remain unbroken. This record is all the more remarkable as he was only 18 when he won his first Open. During the summer of 1875, however, Tom's wife died in childbirth and 'he lost zest for both life and golf'. He was found dead in his bed on Christmas Day that year, aged 24.

Continue along Links Road and pass under the railway. You are now in Station Road where this walk began.

26

CAR OR BICYCLE TOUR OF THE SURROUNDING COUNTRYSIDE AND VILLAGES

The basic circular tour is 24 miles, about an hour's drive if you pause to view places of interest but do not leave the car. The extension to Barnweil in Appendix 1 would add about twenty minutes. The recommended walks would at least double these times; to enjoy them fully would take longer. Enthusiastic visitors may wish to take the tour in sections. To do justice to all of the walks at Auchincruive alone could take several half days.

From Prestwick Station drive through Prestwick towards Ayr. Once past St Nicholas Church, you pass between houses of mixed use in the area known as Prestwick Toll. The main road is here called Ayr Road. Take a right turn into Maryborough Road, immediately before the prominent church on the right - **St Ninian's Episcopal Church** - and park on the road close to the church. It was consecrated in 1926, though the congregation began as a mission formed in 1923.

Close to St Ninian's Church is **Bruce's Well**. Steps lead down into the well, where an inscription records that it was restored in 1912. Beside the well are the sketchy ruins of the Chapel of St Ninian. The chapel may have been founded by missionaries from Whithorn, attracted by supposedly healing waters of a well. 'Spetelcrag' was listed in the Dalmilling Charter (about 1219-1230), indicating that there may have been a spittal (a hospital or leper house) attached to the chapel.

Many believe that King Robert I (Robert the Bruce), who suffered from a form of leprosy, benefited from the healing waters of the well, and this connection may have influenced the name Kingcase, although the original name may have been Kilcase or Kincase. A few months before his death in 1329 the king made a pilgrimage to Whithorn and may have visited Kingcase on the way. He gave the lands of Spittalshiels (Shields) in St Quivox, and Robertlone (Loans) in Dundonald to provide the hospital with an income.

In the 15th century the Wallaces of Craigie retained the right to appoint the head of the hospital and decide who could live there. Although those living at the spittal were described as lepers, many would have suffered from other ailments. They were lodged in huts or cottages and supported by rents. In 1693 the lepers were allowed to gather timber and wrack (seaweed) from the shore, dig peats and collect other materials 'for building and repairing their houses without liberty asked'.

Continue either on foot or by car. There is some parking, and space to turn at the foot of this cul-de-sac. Very obvious, just to the north here, are the **Salt Pan Houses**. Although long disused, these two stone-and-slate buildings are among the best-preserved relics of the salt industry in Scotland. They are believed to date from about 1765, shortly after Richard Oswald of Auchincruive acquired that estate (see p.33).

Salt Pan Houses

Salt was an important commodity and much used to preserve meat for winter use in the days before refrigeration. Before methods of producing it in large quantities were devised in the 19th century its production was a long and laborious business. It was obtained by evaporation of seawater, necessarily at coastal sites. At Prestwick seawater was brought in at high tide and trapped in reservoirs cut in the rock. It was then carried to these buildings, each of which has a vaulted ground floor, where the water was boiled off in iron pans by fires beneath. The fuel, known as pan-coal, came from local pits. The salt produced was of poor quality and used for domestic purposes. On the upper floors, reached only by an external stair, there was living accommodation for the salters and their families. At this time, salters lived in a state of semi-feudalism, being, like colliers, considered as part of the chattels of the estate, to be bought and sold. It is known that in 1470 saltpans near Kingcase were held by Thomas Crawford, whose father was laird of Previk (Privick) a small estate in Tarbolton parish. In 1765 Richard Oswald of Auchincruive obtained from the Freemen of Prestwick 'liberty for erecting a salt pan, one or more, on the sea coast within the liberty of the town of Prestwick, with some grounds for building houses on and yeards for the salters and other workers'. By 1776 management of the pans at Craigie-Maryburgh was in the hands of the Caddells. During the 18th century there was an increase in production of salt in Scotland. Saltpans are known to have been operated locally at Bellrock in 1720 (John Guthrie) and 1750 (Robert Wilson), and there were other panhouses at Bentfield, Bellrock Pit and at Newton on Ayr. Scottish salt was of poor quality and unsuitable for curing fish. Better quality salt was amongst the commodities smuggled into the country in the late 18th century, until changes in taxation brought down its price and destroyed the Scottish salt industry.

Return to the Ayr Road and, taking care, turn right. You soon reach Prestwick Toll, shortly after passing the prominent Centrum and a supermarket. **The Centrum** is a leisure centre that opened in 1996. It has a shop and café, both open to the public, and incorporates a (very visible) private membership health and fitness club.

Turn left immediately after the supermarket, and a set of pedestrian lights, into Waterloo Road. Pause here to look, briefly, at **Kingcase Church**. The Church began as a mission hall in 1912: it became a church in 1934, and a parish church in 1950. A hall was built using voluntary labour in 1949, and the church was substantially extended in 1955-56.

This area is known as **Prestwick Toll**, and is at the boundary between Prestwick and Newton on Ayr. In 1814, 12 small plots were feued for building at Prestwick Toll, to create 'a modern-built village for mechanics'. By 1841 'New Prestwick' had 313 inhabitants, who were mostly employed as weavers, sewers, coalminers and quarriers. Coal mining was carried on in the early 19th century at the Williamfield Pit at Bellrock and the Ann Pit at Heathfield. Prestwick Toll was redeveloped in the 1960s, and many of the original properties, including the original Toll Bar, were demolished.

The Ayrshire Turnpike Act of 1767 designated the road between Ayr and Kilmarnock as one for improvement. The Act enabled Turnpike Trusts to construct and maintain roads. They erected turnpike gates where tolls were collected from road users to cover the cost of building and maintaining the roads. During the mid 19th century, the charge was 4d for a spring-wheeled vehicle, and 3d for a cart. Tolls were abolished in 1878. A small house was provided for the toll-keeper, and a small community grew up here, perhaps encouraged by the keeper's tendency to supplement his income by the sale of spirituous liquors. Mark Kerr, toll-keeper in 1867, paid £337 at the annual auction for the right to collect tolls and occupy the tollhouse.

From Prestwick Toll drive south on the A79. Almost immediately a sign announces that you have left Prestwick and are now in Ayr. At the next set of traffic lights, turn left into Heathfield Road.

One of the shops at the junction of Prestwick Road and Heathfield Road was formerly a bicycle shop run by Graham Obree. It was here that he developed his revolutionary streamlined bicycle. In July 1993 with this bicycle, which famously included parts of an old washing machine, he broke the world record for the greatest distance covered in one hour.

Follow Heathfield Road: on the left you will see, set well back, **Heathfield Primary School**, opened in 1931. Opposite are the remaining buildings of Heathfield Hospital.

Heathfield Hospital was opened in 1904 for the treatment of all notifiable diseases except smallpox and cholera. The fever wards had until then been at Ayr County Hospital. Heathfield could accommodate 60 patients. By the mid-20th century infectious cases had been transferred elsewhere and Heathfield became a general hospital. After the opening of the new Ayr Hospital, all the patients were transferred there. Heathfield closed in 1991, though the out-patients' department is still in use. The X-ray department is used for patients referred by their own GPs. An ante-natal clinic is also held here. The rest of the buildings have been demolished and replaced by houses.

Continue along Heathfield Road, negotiating two roundabouts, giving access to do-it-yourself warehouses, carpet warehouses and the like: the modern insignia of the edge of most towns. At the second roundabout, Liberator Drive leads down to the Ayr Retail Park. This is on part of the site of the **former Ayr airfield**, and is worth a brief pause. Restaurants of the type invariably associated with such developments are also situated here.

The airfield was built as a fighter station for the defence of western Scotland. It opened in April 1941 when the Spitfires of 602 Squadron flew in from Prestwick. Many squadrons were based here in the course of the war to rest out of the front line or to re-equip. The airfield was also the eastern base of the Return Ferry Service (see p.48), which carried pilots and other aircrew back to Canada. On 14th August 1941 a Liberator crashed on take-off, killing all 22 men aboard. The Return Ferry Service and the tragedy are commemorated in the name Liberator Road. In September 1944 RAF Ayr was transferred to the Royal Navy as HMS Wagtail, and served as a shore base for disembarked squadrons. The airfield closed in 1946 and has now largely vanished under housing estates and a Retail Park. The last remaining wartime building is a much-modified hangar now used as a seed store. This is on the eastern edge of the airfield and is best seen from the A77.

Continue along Heathfield Road until it meets the A77 at a roundabout where five roads meet. Take the exit for the B743, signed 'Mauchline'. After half a mile or so you will see the **Hannah Research Institute** on the left, and pass its entrance.

The Hannah Research Institute was opened in 1928 to study the problems that existed in all branches of the dairy industry. Gaps existed in the knowledge of the nutritional requirements of cattle, milk yields and diseases such as tuberculosis and mastitis in the dairy stock. The public milk supply fell far below today's standards. Though milk was a highly nutritious food, it was also a potential carrier of disease. The Institute is named after John M. Hannah, farmer of Girvan Mains, who gifted the Auchincruive estate, including this site, to the nation. Set in famous dairy country, close to the agricultural college and Glasgow's research facilities, it was well placed to raise the quality of milk dramatically over the years.

Continuing along the B743, take the first turning on the left. This leads down to **St Quivox**, a hamlet nestling around an attractive parish church, the whole forming a peaceful retreat from the busy main roads. There is one parking space at the church gates: otherwise cars can be parked carefully on the church side of the road.

About 1220 Walter Fitzalan the High Steward encouraged the Gilbertine monks of the Order of Sempringham from Lincolnshire to found a priory at Dalmilling within the extensive parish of St Quivox. To assist them he gave them the revenues from the parish church and lands and properties within the parish. The attempt failed, the monks returned south in 1238, and the revenues were transferred to Paisley Abbey. The church was restored in 1595 by Alan, Lord Cathcart, who was the owner of the Sundrum and Auchincruive estates and, as laird of Auchincruive, patron of St Quivox Church. This restoration is marked by a stone panel on the outside south wall of the older part of the church, bearing this date, and the Cathcart arms and motto: 'I Hope to Speed.' In 1765 Richard Oswald of Auchincruive, who was then patron, presented Communion cups to the church, which, though not stored in the church for security reasons, are still in use. In 1767 he added a new Auchincruive Gallery with an underlying burial vault, where Oswald is buried. The church retains its box pews and ladles are still used to take up the collection.

In the churchyard the most prominent feature is the **Mausoleum**, with Doric columns, raised in 1822 by the Campbells of Craigie. This was designed by the Edinburgh architect William Henry Playfair. There are also a number of old and unusual tombstones in the churchyard, with one, at least, dating back to 1657, and many others from the 18th Century. In the village are a number of attractive typical old cottages, and the two-storey former Manse, with bay windows extending through both floors and a central doorway with columns. Just outside the village (on the right as you came in, and on the left as you leave) is **Mount Hamilton**, another substantial late 18th century house, though it incorporates an older structure. Now used for student accommodation, this was the house (and office) of factors on the Auchincruive estate.

St Quivox Church

From St Quivox return to the B743, turn right, and almost immediately take the first turn on the left. This road passes farm and academic buildings of the Auchincruive Campus of the **Scottish Agricultural College**. After half a mile, and just before a narrow bridge, there is a public entrance to the estate. Turn in, and please take care to repay the warm welcome by keeping your wheels well away from the carefully tended grass. There is a large car park on the left, close to the mansion house now known as **Oswald Hall**. You are invited to walk over most of the estate, avoiding the working farms and academic buildings.

The interior of the house is well worth seeing, especially the Adam ceilings, and the fireplaces and door-casings. Enter the main door and turn right into Reception. You will be directed to any of the principal rooms that are not occupied by conferences. In 1927 the estate became the West of Scotland Agricultural College, which in 1990 merged into the Scottish Agricultural College. It offers many courses on a wide variety of rural subjects at several levels, from school leaver to postgraduate.

You can ask at Reception for a copy of the free leaflet *Country Walks Around Auchincruive, Annbank and Mossblown*, which includes a map. It is also available from libraries and tourist information centres.

You can take several walks through the estate. We shall describe a few. The first visits the Temple or Teahouse and the Icehouse. Walk past the front of the Hall and up the main drive. If it is not convenient to walk, you can drive most of the way and use the Refectory car park.

If you are walking, you can cross the stile on your right, almost hidden by a rhododendron almost 50 yards beyond the sign 'Mansionfield'. Follow the path through the woodland to a Y-junction and turn left for the Teahouse. If you wish to visit the Icehouse, used to preserve food through the warm seasons, first go right at the junction and then downhill for a few yards. The pond that supplied the ice is a few yards beyond it. Return to the junction and turn right to leave the wood.

The path rejoins the drive opposite the Cunningham Building. Turn right past Gibbsyard, the splendid former farm steading on your left, and walk on to the Refectory area on your right. At the far end of this enclosure there is a signboard headed 'Auchincruive Robert Adam Tea House Restoration', and to its left is a walkway leading to this building. The Teahouse, built in 1780, was probably influenced by the Mausoleum of Theodoric in Ravenna. On the upper floor of the Teahouse the Oswald family could take tea and admire the view. You may care to take in this view yourself, from ground level, before walking back to the Hall.

Follow the drive around the right-hand side of the Hall. At the corner is an ancient Holm Oak. On your right, close to the big rhododendron, is a pets' cemetery, with headstones of 1861 and 1872 in memory of a horse and a squirrel. Look over the railings for a sweeping view of the river, and below you the Hanging Gardens. These are a huge retaining wall, built in terraces by unemployed miners in 1830.

The interior of the house is well worth seeing, especially the Adam ceilings, and the fireplaces and door-casings. Enter the main door and turn right into Reception. You will be directed to any of the principal rooms that are not occupied by conferences. In 1927 the estate became the West of Scotland Agricultural College, which in 1990 merged into the Scottish Agricultural College. It offers many courses on a wide variety of rural subjects at several levels, from school leaver to postgraduate.

You can ask at Reception for a copy of the free leaflet *Country Walks Around Auchincruive, Annbank and Mossblown*, which includes a map. It is also available from libraries and tourist information centres.

You can take several walks through the estate. We shall describe a few. The first visits the Temple or Teahouse and the Icehouse. Walk past the front of the Hall and up the main drive. If it is not convenient to walk, you can drive most of the way and use the Refectory car park.

If you are walking, you can cross the stile on your right, almost hidden by a rhododendron almost 50 yards beyond the sign 'Mansionfield'. Follow the path through the woodland to a Y-junction and turn left for the Teahouse. If you wish to visit the Icehouse, used to preserve food through the warm seasons, first go right at the junction and then downhill for a few yards. The pond that supplied the ice is a few yards beyond it. Return to the junction and turn right to leave the wood.

The path rejoins the drive opposite the Cunningham Building. Turn right past Gibbsyard, the splendid former farm steading on your left, and walk on to the Refectory area on your right. At the far end of this enclosure there is a signboard headed 'Auchincruive Robert Adam Tea House Restoration', and to its left is a walkway leading to this building. The Teahouse, built in 1780, was probably influenced by the Mausoleum of Theodoric in Ravenna. On the upper floor of the Teahouse the Oswald family could take tea and admire the view. You may care to take in this view yourself, from ground level, before walking back to the Hall.

Follow the drive around the right-hand side of the Hall. At the corner is an ancient Holm Oak. On your right, close to the big rhododendron, is a pets' cemetery, with headstones of 1861 and 1872 in memory of a horse and a squirrel. Look over the railings for a sweeping view of the river, and below you the Hanging Gardens. These are a huge retaining wall, built in terraces by unemployed miners in 1830.

Oswald Hall

Walk towards the house. The older part of this mansion was completed in 1767 by Richard Oswald using designs by the architect Robert Adam. It was extended in the late 19th century, but some of Adam's work remains.

Richard Oswald (1705-1784), the son of a Caithness minister, began his business career in Glasgow. He was a successful entrepreneur in the Atlantic trade, shipping slaves from Africa to America and the West Indies, and bringing back cotton, sugar and tobacco to Glasgow. His company's trading station at Bance Island, Sierra Leone, was one of the biggest in Africa: here Oswald's agents kept and transshipped slaves, and negotiated their business with the local chiefs. Oswald also had estates in Jamaica, Florida and South Carolina, and his second wife, Mary Ramsay, inherited further estates in Jamaica. Oswald's wealth enabled him to buy the Auchincruive estate, where he threw himself enthusiastically into estate improvement, and involvement in the local community. He also developed the industrial potential of his land, especially through coal mining. The American War of Independence affected his American estates, including those he had acquired following his appointment as Commissary General (supplier of goods) to the British Army during the Seven Years' War (1756-1763). The conclusion of the War of Independence gave him a chance to make a mark on history. He had been a friend and business associate of Benjamin Franklin, and the British government and the American colonists found Oswald a suitable intermediary to negotiate the peace conditions that culminated in the Treaty of Paris (1783). Oswald engineered a peace that did not leave scars or unsolved problems that could have led to further conflicts.

The Hanging Gardens

A wide footpath leads down to the river, and to a pleasant riverside and woodland walk of up to 3 miles. This is shown in the leaflet previously mentioned as the 'Oswald Trail', but we shall add a little to the necessarily brief description there.

When you reach the riverbank look downstream for another view of the Hanging Gardens.

Walk upstream, and you will soon pass the College's formal gardens, with greenhouses behind. If you wish to visit them, take the next turn to the left, walk to the top of the slope and you will find gates. There are many fine trees here, including a many-trunked Japanese Red Cedar, probably 200 years old, roughly in the middle of the garden. The gardens and glasshouses continue a pattern begun by Richard Oswald, who was one of the first in Scotland to build hothouses for figs, vines, sugar cane and pineapples. If you wish to see inside them, ask any member of the gardening staff.

There are toilets in the building nearest to the Hall.

Continuing along the riverside, you are almost sure to see mallards, occasionally the stately goosander or the kingfisher, and the grey wagtail, the dipper and the grey heron standing on stones. A little way upstream the river is almost dammed by a line of rocks. This is a dyke: molten rock has been thrust through a crack and solidified to form a wall. Since this rock is harder than the rest, it has resisted erosion by the river better, and stands above it.

After passing through a kissing gate, you enter deciduous woodland. Continuing upstream you will pass under the water pipe, and later pass cliffs of shale on your left. Occasionally small falls of this soft rock are imprinted with the fossil traces of carboniferous plants, reminding us that coal mining was important in this area for much of the 18th, 19th and 20th centuries. Further upstream you will see the impressive stone piers of a viaduct that carried a tramway on which horses drew waggons of coal, from left to right as you face, from the mines around Annbank to Ayr for export by sea.

(This is a convenient place to turn back if you wish to avoid a steeper though rewarding route above the river valley.)

Pass through a gateway in a stone wall and follow the riverbank: there is a marker post after a few yards and another close to the end of the viaduct. There are several paths to the left which you might explore on a future visit. Pass Brockle Quarry, now disused and flooded, below on your left, and walk up the hillside, away from the river until you meet a T-junction. The path to the right leads to Annbank (p.37), but we turn left and walk on until we meet a minor public road. Turn left into it and in about ¼ mile pass through a wooden gate on the left. You have re-entered the estate at the **Arboretum**, where over a thousand trees, all different and all labelled, are planted in formal lines. They are there for educational purposes, and are grouped according to their landscaping or horticultural uses. This Arboretum was planted in the mid-1980s, and all the trees were sponsored by individuals or organisations. You can either join a track just ahead or stroll along the numerous green paths which run parallel to it and enjoy the trees.

In either case you will meet a metalled drive, with the East Lodge and Nellie's Gate (believed to be named after an early gate-keeper), on your right and the Ayr-to-Mauchline road behind it. Turn right and almost immediately left into another drive or, if you wish, pass through a gate into another part of the Arboretum, and rejoin the drive later. Walk forward, and shortly you will see the playing fields on your left and soon reach Oswald Hall and your parked car.

Before driving away, or on future visits, you may like to take one or more of the following walks.

Just outside the entrance to the estate the road crosses the River Ayr by **Oswald's Bridge**, a substantial stone structure with round pedestrian refuges. On your right just after the bridge you will find a path leading, in a few steps, to the **Leglen Wood Monument**. Built of Ailsa Craig granite in 1929, it commemorates the association with this area of the Scots patriot Sir William Wallace and the poet Robert Burns. From here a path leads to another pleasant riverside walk. Back on the road a few more steps bring you to crumbling stone walls on either side, just before a smallholding. Here one of the 18th-century horse waggonways built to carry coal to Ayr, much of it for shipping to Ireland, passed under the road through a tunnel which still exists. (For a more detailed account of the waggonways see Harry Broad's *Rails to Ayr*, published by the AANHS in 1981.)

From here turn back, either to return to your car or to take one of the waymarked walks shown in the aforementioned leaflet. Two of them go off to the right just before the bridge. The Waggonway Trail (3 miles) visits Wallace's Seat, a rocky viewpoint overlooking the River Ayr, and passes though a very impressive cutting made for the waggonway. The Three Green Knights Trail (1½ miles) is a shorter walk giving good views of the Estate and Hall. To reach the Farm Trail, pass the Estate entrance and continue up the road to a signpost indicating a cycle route to Ayr. Follow this and cross a stile into the wood, and follow the markers. Part of this walk is on the old stagecoach road to Ayr.

On leaving Auchincruive by car, turn left and cross Oswald's Bridge. (In the evening if the gate is locked drive back in front of the Hall and follow the drive to the main exit.) After a mile or so turn left at a T-junction, which has poor visibility, and head towards Annbank. This road crosses the river Ayr again, at **Tarholm Bridge**, a concrete bridge of 1930, before entering the former mining village of Annbank.

If you wish to stroll along the banks of the Ayr, you can park on the right just before the bridge and enter the gate on your right just beyond it.

Although there is now nothing to be seen of the works, here at Tarholm in the 1780s the British Tar Company distilled tar from coal, using a process invented by Archibald Cochrane, the 9th Earl of Dundonald (1748-1831), one of the foremost industrial chemists of his day.

Annbank originated about 1860 to house workers at the pits then being developed on the Enterkine estate by the Ayr Coal Company (George Taylor & Co). The first houses, typical miners' rows with a minimum of facilities, were replaced during the 1930s by Ayr County Council, and it is these houses which form the bulk of the modern village.

The street through Annbank is exceptionally wide. When the miners' rows were being replaced by the present houses, the new buildings were erected immediately behind the old ones, which were then evacuated and demolished.

A visitor to Annbank in 1863 found 'houses, which are built of brick, being one-storey and ranged on either side of the road, no provision of a sanitary nature seems to be provided, as directly in front of each door there stands a heap of ashes and filth, and betwixt each there are large pools of green stagnant water which rises and falls according to the weather, a perfect hotbed for fever and other diseases.' The visit had been occasioned by a strike, for the miners of Annbank were among the most militant in opposing the iniquitous truck system, by which they were paid in tokens that could only be spent in a store belonging to the coal company (see *Ayrshire Miners' Rows, 1913*, published by the AANHS.)

The best-known son of Annbank is James Brown, who started life as a miner, and rose to become a highly respected MP. He is commemorated by a monument (1954) on your left in the centre of the village.

The route continues through Annbank and drops down a hill to a staggered crossroads. On your right you can see the Victorian lodge and gates of the Enterkine estate. Enterkine House was built in an American style in 1939, replacing an earlier house, and is now a hotel and restaurant.

At the staggered junction turn right and then immediately left. This is the B744 which, after a mile joins the B743. At the junction stop and turn right. Almost immediately, turn left towards Tarbolton on what is, again, the B744.

In a mile or so, you enter the village of **Tarbolton.** At a junction, marked by the Peterhead granite **War Memorial** of 1920, turn left. The village is worth exploring. It is an ancient settlement which in the late 18th century became a thriving weaving centre and the heart of a fertile farming area. Later, coal mining became the major industry. Today it is mainly a dormitory for people employed in Ayr, Kilmarnock and other towns.

Tarbolton Parish Church

Although it is impossible to verify, the name Tarbolton is believed locally to derive from tor (a hill), Baal (a pagan god) and ton (a settlement).

There is public parking close to the Activity Centre: this is on the left as you drive down the main street. Its sign is on your right. The tower of the Parish Church overlooks the carpark. If you stand with your back to it, you will see the **Erskine Hall**, built in 1778 as the (Secession) Erskine Church. After a series of re-unifications its congregation was united with that of the Parish Church in 1943, and this building became a public hall..

Leave your car there and turn left in the main street. At once on your right is the **Lorimer Library and Institute.** It is named after John Lorimer, a Glasgow businessman who died in 1877, and who left money for it in his Will. He had been brought up in Tarbolton and made a great deal of money in America. The Library was opened in 1878, and is now run as part of South Ayrshire Council's library service. In it is a map that shows Tarbolton's history.

It is open on Tuesdays and Fridays 2.30 to 4.30, and 5.00 to 7.00, and on Mondays and Thursdays in the afternoon only

At the cross-roads which marks the centre of the village, turn left. Opposite the Crown Inn are the substantial gates of **Tarbolton Parish Church**. This building of 1821 replaced an older church. There are graves of Covenanters and victims of pit accidents. At the centre of the outside rear wall of the church is the gravestone of Dr Patrick Woodrow, the Minister of Tarbolton Church when Burns and his family worshipped there. Woodrow is mentioned unflatteringly, and his assistant the Rev. John McMath kindly, in Burns' poem 'The Twa Herds', and in the 'Epistle to the Rev. John McMath'.

Leave the churchyard by the same entrance and turn left. Follow the graveyard wall as it curves left into Kirkgate, where the former manse faces you. The grounds have been developed in the 1990s for housing, but this informal classical house, built in 1792, still has a commanding presence. Return to the village cross, and turn left into Burn Street. On the right is the **Town House** of Tarbolton. This simple two-storey building was erected in 1832. It has an external stair to the Council Chamber and a walled-up former entrance to the gaol. The Burgh Council still meets here once a year, at Yuletide. Before the meeting the Bellboy (an office handed down from father to son) announces it through the streets. The meeting chooses the new Council, two bailies and twelve councillors. This concludes the business for the year.

> Charles II created Tarbolton a Free Burgh of Barony in 1671, giving it the privilege of holding markets and fairs. The aim was to encourage trade and to persuade tradesmen to settle here. When most Burghs in Scotland became Police Burghs after 1862, Tarbolton chose not to, although this robbed the Burgh Council of most of its powers.

Continue to the bottom of Burn Street. A plaque in the garden of the house at the junction records that this was the **site of James Manson's Inn,** where the St James Lodge of Freemason met, and that Manson was their Treasurer. Robert Burns was originally a member of St David's Lodge, and when it merged with the St James Lodge in 1784 Burns became the Depute Master, until he moved away to Mossgiel Farm near Mauchline. During 1787 and 1788 the Master was James Dalrymple of Orangefield (see p.45 and 49), and he was succeeded by Burns' friend Gavin Hamilton.

Turn right here into Garden Street, the B744. Shortly you will meet a narrow road climbing a steep hill on your left. This leads to **Hoodshill,** named after John Hood, a local schoolmaster in the mid 18th century, who rented it for his pupils' recreation. Hoodshill is all that remains of a castle mound (motte) and flat fortified enclosure (bailey) dating from the 12th century. It may have been constructed by Gilbert, son of Richer, to whom the lands of Tarbolton were granted by Walter the High Steward. If you wish to view it at close quarters walk up the road, but a more impressive view can be seen by continuing along the B744 for three or four minutes and looking back at the hill.

Another three minutes' walk will bring you to a plaque in the hedge on your right commemorating the imaginary meeting, described by Burns, of Dr Hornbook and Death. John Wilson, the schoolmaster of the village, the Dr Hornbook of the poem, treated the local people's ailments. Death complains that he has been cheated of his conquests, as the medicines of Dr Hornbook have killed his patients first!

The house a little further along on your right is on the site of **Willie's Mill**, mentioned in Burns' poetry and writings. The former mill was driven by the Water of Fail.

The B744 continues past **Lochlea Farm,** on its way to Galston. The Burns family lived there from 1777 to 1784, and Robert would have travelled this road regularly. But our route takes us back to the village centre and turns left into Sandgate. Immediately on the right, in a thatched 17th-century building, is the **Bachelors' Club**, with its strong associations with Burns. It now belongs to the National Trust for Scotland and is open regularly during the summer.

Robert Burns was instrumental in setting up the Bachelors' Club in 1780. It consisted of Burns, who became its president, his brother Gilbert and five other young men. It was a literary and debating society and the first motion discussed was whether one should marry for looks or for fortune. In Burns' time the building was also the village hall. It was here that Burns attended dancing classes and also where he became a mason in 1781.

Outside the Bachelors' Club turn left, then left again at the village cross, and pass the Lorimer Library. This street, **Montgomerie Street,** has most of Tarbolton's facilities, including a post office, a grocery and a cafe. On the opposite side, about 100 yards past the Library, is the present day **Masonic Lodge, St James.** This contains many Burns relics, and can often be visited by previous arrangement with the Secretary, telephone 01290-551100.

Return from here to the Activity Centre and your car.

Leave Tarbolton by turning left out of the car park, turning left at the village cross roads, passing the Parish Church, and following Cunningham Street and Croft Street, which form the B730. After the speed de-restriction signs the road curves to the left, and you can see the Barnweil Monument (p.51) on the skyline ahead.

On the right of the road there is a large area of wetland called **Tarbolton Loch**. Until the mid 19th century this was a sheet of water about ¼ mile square, flooded artificially in winter to drive a mill, and drained in summer to grow hay. The stretch of open water near the road is the Burns Trout Fishing. It is open all year round and day tickets are sold at the office. The telephone number is 01292-541509, but booking is not necessary.

After about ¼ mile a small group of buildings comes into sight ahead, a little to the right of the road. This is the site of the House of Fail, a religious foundation.

> **House of Fail**. In 1252 at the ancient ford where the main road from Ayr to Edinburgh crossed the Water of Fail, members of the Order of the Holy Trinity for the Redemption of Captives (often called Trinitarians, or Red Friars) established a small religious community. The main purpose of the Red Friars was to collect funds to ransom prisoners of the Saracens during the Crusades. In addition they provided help for the poor and sick in a spittal beside their House. The House of Fail was the principal Trinitarian House in Scotland and its Minister sat in the Scottish Parliament. Unfortunately the good work of the Red Friars is largely undocumented, and the best known memorial to them is the scurrilous lines:
>
> > *The Friars of fail they made gude kail*
> > *On Friday when they fasted;*
> > *And never wanted gear enough*
> > *As long as their neighbours' lasted.*

In 1561, at the Reformation, the Privy Council ordered the destruction of the House, and little was left except the Minister's accommodation. The last minister appears to have been the Episcopalian Walter Whiteford, who later became Bishop of Brechin, but was deposed and fled to England, where he died in 1643. The ruins of the building survived until 1952, when the stones were taken away for road-bottoming around Prestwick Airport. A few stones were saved and were used to make a small grotto in the grounds of the Roman Catholic Church in Mossblown.

Continue along the road to a T-junction, passing on your left a white cottage, Fail Toll, a reminder of turnpike roads.

If you want to visit the Barnweil Monument and Barnweil Church and take a scenic route, go to Appendix 1. You will pass along very narrow, winding lanes, which demand great care and low speeds.

If you want to avoid these turn left onto the A719. After almost 2 miles fork right onto the B739. After a further 1½ miles you will pass the entrance to **Adamton House**.

Adamton House

The present red sandstone house, with its curved gables reminiscent of Dutch architecture, was built in 1885 for the new owner of the estate, John George Alexander Baird MP. It changed hands frequently during the 20th century. Adamton served as accommodation for American servicemen stationed at Prestwick throughout the Second World War and into the 1960s. After lying empty for several years it was licensed in 1973 as a hotel, and became well known for its 'medieval' banquets. In 1986 British Aerospace took it over and extended it to provide student accommodation for the Flying College at Prestwick, which could train 120 students at a time. In the 1990s the flying college was relocated to Spain, and in 2003 Adamton House is again empty.

Beyond Adamton House the B739 passes under the Ayr by-pass. After half a mile or so, the road passes **HMS Gannet**, a Naval Air Station. The site had been used by the United States Air Force for twenty years until the mid 1960s.

In 1971, 819 Squadron of the Royal Navy was re-formed at HMS Gannet with Sea King helicopters in the anti-submarine role for the defence of the Clyde. It also undertook many search-and-rescue operations, including the Piper Alpha and Lockerbie tragedies (both 1988). The Squadron was de-commissioned in November 2001. HMS Gannet now houses a Search and Rescue Flight equipped with three Sea King Mark 5 helicopters. The operational area covers 81,000 square miles, extending from Ben Nevis to the Lake District, and from the Borders to a position 200 miles into the Atlantic. The crews are highly trained in immediate emergency care. Each year they respond to 250 or more calls for help.

On the left-hand side of the road are many ancillary buildings associated with the BAE Systems factory. On the ridge above the road on the right are an old windmill or doocot and **Macrae's Monument**.

Macrae's Monument

The Monument is worth a closer look; it has Corinthian columns and friezes depicting ships, anchors, dolphins etc. To visit it, turn into the next lane on your right, signed 'Whiteside'. This lane turns to the right just in front of the farm buildings. A metalled road and a car park close to the monument are planned but were not installed at the time of writing. If they are still not completed you can park on the right just round the corner, near to a gate in the stone wall. Continue along the lane on foot and you will soon arrive at the monument.

James Macrae was a local boy made good. He was born at Ochiltree about 1674 and was brought up in Ayr by his mother, a washerwoman. He was encouraged to go to sea by a carpenter named McGuire, who had befriended him, and he entered the service of the East India Company. He rose to become Governor of Madras in 1725 and made his fortune as a merchant. He left India in 1731 worth £100,000, which was then a vast fortune. On his return to Ayrshire he rewarded the relations of his early benefactor. At Monkton he built a large house, which he called Orangefield in honour of William of Orange, and he died there in 1744.

During restoration of the monument in 2000-2001, the skeletons of two men, two women and two children were found interred within it. Only two coffins were intact: the bones of the others were mixed up, and there was evidence of disturbance, possibly in the early 20th century. The style of the coffins suggested a date in the late 18th century. It is not known whose remains they were. The bones were re-interred.

The road ends in a junction with the road to Kilmarnock; turn left towards the centre of the village of **Monkton** and at the traffic lights take the second exit faced by the Wheatsheaf Inn. There is a car park opposite the Inn, and another immediately beyond it. It is advisable to park and visit the various places of interest on foot.

Monkton is a small village, but until early in the 19th century its population was not much smaller than that of Prestwick. Its farms were richer, and it was surrounded by more large estates.

In the centre of the village is the Muckle Stane, a seven-ton glacial erratic boulder recently saved from destruction and relocated at Monkton Cross through the efforts of Monkton Historical Society. Near by is the **Carvick Webster Hall**, opened in 1929.

The hall was given to the villagers of Monkton by Harry and Agnes Carvick Webster of Orangefield (see above) as a memorial to their two sons, John and Harry, who died serving with the Army: John in

Mesopotamia (Iraq) in 1917, and Harry on the North West Frontier (Pakistan) in 1923. It is a thorough reconstruction of the original Monkton and Prestwick Free Church, opened in 1843. This was one of the earliest Free Churches to be completed following the Disruption.

Opposite the Wheatsheaf are the **remains of St Cuthbert's parish church**. The oblong body of the church is medieval – its richly decorated south door has been dated to the 13th century. A wing was added after the Reformation, and is now the burial place of the Angus family of Ladykirk.

Before the Reformation churches such as this were very colourful places, designed for worship centred on one or more altars and distancing the officiating clergy from the congregation. After the Reformation they were altered to give emphasis to the preacher and to gather the congregation as near as possible to the pulpit. Very little remains in the building to recall either of these arrangements.

The graveyard contains the graves of several prominent local families and has some Burns associations. The poet Blind Harry tells us that William Wallace's dream, telling him that he was to be the Guardian of the Covenant of Scotland, came to him in the churchyard.

The imposing manse stands immediately behind the church and can be seen from a lane on the right.

This church, and that of St Nicholas in Prestwick, were abandoned when in 1837, during the ministry of the Rev. Thomas Burns, the poet's nephew, a new joint Prestwick and Monkton Parish Church, also dedicated to St Cuthbert, was built between the two villages. Your route will take you to it shortly. After serving there for six years, Thomas Burns supported the Disruption of the Church of Scotland and joined the Free Church. In that year a new Free Church was built, as described under 'Carvick Webster Hall' above. In 1848 he and a party of Free Church emigrants left Scotland for New Zealand, where they founded the provinces of Otago and Southland.

Thomas Burns' successor as minister of new St Cuthbert's in 1843 was the Rev. George James Lawrie, who had been a chaplain to the East India Company in Madras. He retired in 1838 and settled in Monkton, building Bellary, across the road from old St Cuthbert's. He remained there during his ministry, and did not occupy the manse He was greatly esteemed by his parishioners, even though for the last ten years of his life he suffered severely from fever and was unable to preach.

The road past the church used to be the main Glasgow to Ayr road and at one time went straight across the main airport runway. There were traffic lights to stop road vehicles when an aeroplane was landing or taking off. A road built in the 1960s now takes traffic around the western end of the main runway: we will follow it later. Walk down to where the road goes left to the entrance of the BAE Systems factory (formerly British Aerospace) and you will see the **'Palace'** building on your left (see p.47 and p.56). The terminal buildings of Glasgow Prestwick International Airport can be seen on the other side of the main runway. (For an account of the Airport see Appendix 2.)

Return to your car, go back to the cross and go straight across to the Irvine road (to the left of the Carvick Webster Hall). At the roundabout turn left onto the A79. Just along here on the left, and close to a convenient lay-by, is a small graveyard, the resting place of the Campbells of Fairfield. Alongside the graveyard is a rectangular brick-built enclosure. This was intended as a stable block, part of a failed development, and was left in this folly-like condition.

To the left of the next roundabout is a bronze **statue of a winged man.** It was made by Scott Associates and was the result of a competition among Ayrshire schools (won by Carrick Academy, Maybole) for a feature to mark the entrance to the Prestwick International Aerospace Park. It was erected in 2003.

Continue along the A79, passing under the elevated walkway connecting the Airport to its railway station, which opened in 1994. If you wish to visit the Airport Terminal, at the next roundabout take the first exit. Follow the road in front of the Terminal building and head for the Short Stay, No.2, car park. (Note that there is currently no free car parking at the airport.) Make your way down to the Terminal Building where there are a bar, café and toilets. There is also a viewing balcony from which aeroplane movements can be watched.

Flying in the vicinity of the present-day **Glasgow Prestwick International Airport** started in 1933 when John Sword, a Scottish pioneer of road transport and civil aviation, used a field situated between Monkton and the site of the present Terminal for his Midland and Scottish Air Ferries. The origin of the airport is recognised as being when David McIntyre and Lord Douglas Douglas-Hamilton founded Scottish Aviation Ltd in 1935 (see p.56). One of their intentions was to develop an international airport at Prestwick. The Second World War pushed Prestwick to the fore. In 1940 the Air Ministry designated Prestwick as the eastern terminal for the Atlantic Ferry Organisation, which delivered US and Canadian-built aircraft to the UK, and the first scheduled landplane service across the North Atlantic was started by BOAC in May 1941 to return the air ferry crews to Canada. A major factor in these decisions was Prestwick's exceptional fog-free weather conditions and the facilities provided by Scottish Aviation Ltd (SAL) and it became one of the busiest airfields in the world. In the course of the war Prestwick handled more than 37,000 transatlantic flights, and thousands of other flights within the UK.

Airport Terminal

At its peak of activity there were more than 300 aircraft movements a day. The airfield was also used by the Air Transport Auxiliary (ATA), which delivered aeroplanes from factories to front-line squadrons.

> One of the ATA's best-known pilots was Amy Johnson, whose solo flight from England to Australia in a single-engined biplane in 1930 made her a national heroine. On 4th January 1941 Amy Johnson left Prestwick in an Airspeed Oxford to fly to Kidlington, near Oxford. As with all ATA pilots she flew visually, without radio or radio navigation aids. She landed at Blackpool and visited her sister. Though her journey had been difficult owing to compass problems, she ignored advice to delay her flight to have the compass checked and despite adverse weather she set off again the next morning. Later news came that an aeroplane had crashed into the Thames Estuary and that papers belonging to Amy Johnson had been found. It is likely that she ran out of fuel and baled out. Her body was never recovered.

The first hard runway at Prestwick was constructed in 1941, twice the length and width of the standard runway at the time, and a second was built the following year. The Air Traffic Control Centre for transatlantic flights was moved from Gloucester to Prestwick. Orangefield House, which was built around 1740, was used by Scottish Aviation as part of its Flying Training School and then was developed as the terminal building, with the addition of a control tower on top of its concrete-filled chimney stacks. By October 1944 seven airlines operated services from Prestwick with over 1,000 transatlantic flights per month, and by 1945 it was the best-equipped airport on this side of the Atlantic, with numerous facilities for passengers. It even had an orchestra providing music on Sunday evenings.

After the war the Government decided that Heathrow was to be Britain's main transatlantic airport, and Prestwick was designated the second transatlantic gateway, so maintaining its important position in the civil air transport business with many international airlines, including Scottish Airlines (part of SAL), operating services the world over. Over the years many famous statesmen, royalty, film stars and other celebrities have passed through the airport. Prestwick saw Elvis Presley's only 'visit' to Britain, on 2nd March 1960, as he returned to the USA from army service in Germany. His aeroplane landed to refuel and Elvis met a few of his Scottish fans.

Orangefield House was demolished in 1964, having been superseded by the present Terminal Building (designed by JL Gleave and Partners) which was opened in 1964 by Queen Elizabeth the Queen Mother. In the main concourse is a plaque honouring David McIntyre.

Prestwick's fortunes slipped during the 1960s as aircraft were developed that could fly longer distances and also did not need the long runways at Prestwick. (The main runway is 9800 feet long, the longest in Scotland.) Regular transatlantic scheduled flights declined, with operators such as SAS and KLM leaving in 1968 and 1969 respectively, and a further downturn followed in 1990 when Prestwick's Scottish transatlantic gateway status was abolished. Prestwick has however weathered the lean years, and owing to energetic and committed management, often local, has emerged with a growing air cargo business, many holiday charter flights, and as the Scottish base for Ryanair, one of the largest airlines in Europe.

On leaving the terminal follow the exit signs to the roundabout, noticing on the way a striking steel sculpture, erected in 1997, 'The Celestial Navigator' by Carol Grey.

Take the first exit left towards Prestwick town. At the next roundabout, again go to the first left on to what used to be the main Ayr to Glasgow road, the same one that you were on in Monkton. On your right is the **former Prestwick and Monkton Parish Church**, of 1837, built for the Reverend

Thomas Burns (see p.46), nephew of the poet Robert Burns. Its high cost was much discussed at the time. It is a rather opulent building, with large gargoyles and numerous pinnacles. This church was superseded by Monkton and Prestwick North Parish Church (see p.15). When the congregation moved to the new church they took the bell with them. Just beyond the church the road crosses the Pow Burn by a bridge engraved with the dates 1773 and 1831. Around you are the remains of the old Terminal area, now used by a variety of businesses connected with the airport, and there is little left to see, though names such as McIntyre Avenue and Elvis Street act as reminders of the past.

Return to the roundabout, and take the first exit - signed 'Shawfarm Industrial Estate' - pass under a latticed footbridge, ignore the farm entrance first left, and take the second-left road, signed 'Cemetery'. The lodge and gateway to **Monkton and Prestwick Joint Cemetery** are obvious on the left. A large grey stone marks the grave of John Keppie RSA and three of his sisters. The Cemetery also offers some of the finest views of the activity of the airport.

Continue along Shaw Road past the Cemetery to its end. Park well before the gates of GE Caledonian. From here the **Shaw Tower** can be seen clearly. For a closer view follow the track leading up the grassy bank to the left and between high wire fences. Although records are lacking, the tower is believed to have been built by a local laird for observing falconry. From the base of the tower there is another fine view of the airport.

From here return to the roundabout and take the first exit towards Prestwick. At the traffic lights a right turn will take you back along Station Road to the car park at the railway station.

APPENDIX 1

Visits to Barnweil Monument and Barnweil Church

This route follows some narrow twisting roads needing extra care and low speeds.

At the junction of the B730 and the A719, near Fail Toll (see p.42) turn right, signed 'Galston', and after about ½ mile turn into the B730, signed 'Dundonald'. After a little over ½ mile turn left; a signpost indicates 'Barnweil Monument'. The roads for the next five miles or so are narrow and have few passing places. They demand an extremely low speed and a sharp look-out, but the views are most rewarding

Wallace Monument, Barnweil

Take a left fork at a house named Barnweil, built about 1810. This was the home of General James George Smith Neill of Swinridgemuir, who fought and

51

died in the Indian Mutiny (1857), and is commemorated by a statue in Wellington Square, Ayr (see *Historic Ayr* p.33). Continue to the Barnweil Monument, which is now in sight. You are invited to park in the yard of the farmstead of 'Hill of Barnweil'. Drive right in and park near the left or right wall, clear of doorways. At the time of writing it is not safe to go to the top of the Monument, but much can be seen from the foot. We cannot do better than quote the words of the plaque near the door: 'The tower, designed and erected by the builder and mason Robert Snodgrass, was erected in 1855 by one William Patrick of Roughwood. It was a tribute to William Wallace, "Guardian of Scotia". It is one of a series of Wallace Monuments built throughout the country in the 19th century.' From the tower the whole of the Ayrshire landscape, coast and Firth of Clyde can be seen.

The vista is truly impressive. It includes parts of the Highlands and the Southern Uplands, large parts of the Central Lowlands, and much of the Clyde estuary. To see it all, you will need to move about the Monument's enclosure, and into the field behind the barn, through two gates, closing them after you. The Viewfinder on page 54 will help you identify some of the landmarks which you can see in clear weather.

Returning down the road, bear left at the T-junction, at the 'No Through Road' sign of Hall of Barnweil Farm on the right, then take the first turn left. Just after a crossroads you can park (two cars) on the grass verge on the left. Opposite is a short length of fence, which the farmer has arranged to be suitable for climbing. Please do not take dogs with you. Walk not to the summit of the hill but to its left, and you will meet an impressive ditch surrounding a motte, an artificial hill on which a defended building was built in the Middle Ages. It is rectangular: they are usually round. To your left, parallel humps and depressions in the ground remain from old ridge-and-furrow cultivation. The other earthworks in this field probably result from quarrying.

Go back over the fence, and walk right down the road, to a rock face at a gateway, a former quarry. Passing through the gate, you will soon reach the **ruins of Barnweil Church**, in a cluster of trees. The parish of Barnweil was abolished in 1673, one of the few in Ayrshire to suffer this fate, and its lands were divided between the parishes of Craigie and Tarbolton. This is a good example of a common arrangement: a church (earlier than the present building) on high ground within a few hundred yards of a fortified home.

Return to your car, and descend the hill. At the give-way sign at the bottom turn left, and almost immediately turn left again, between a farm steading and a bungalow. Enjoying the changing vista, continue about a mile and turn right at the T-junction. After another ½ mile turn left at the next junction. From here on, several lay-bys or passing places permit a brief stop to admire the view of uplands, Prestwick and Ayr, and the airport. In less than a mile turn right at the T-junction. Our idyll is ended: we are again on a two-way road! This is the B739, leading us under the A77 to Monkton. After two miles or so, this road passes the entrance to Adamton House. The house itself can be seen from the A77.

Here we rejoin the main route on p.43.

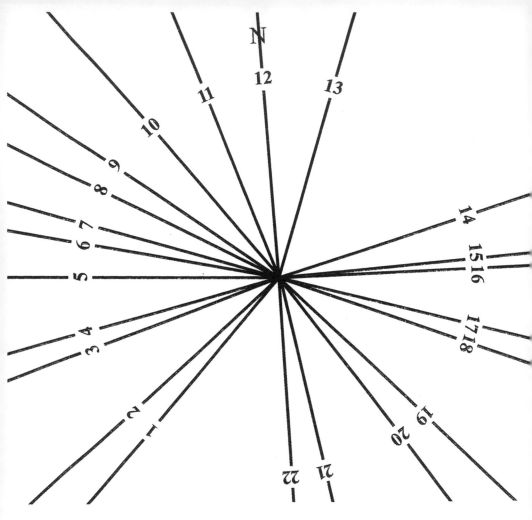

To use the **viewfinder**, lay it on a horizontal surface such as a gatepost and align the appropriate line with any unmistakable landmark. All of the other lines will then point correctly. Or line up the magnetic north line 'N' with the needle of a compass.

Looking leftward along the coast you meet Prestwick, Ayr and the Heads of Ayr. Returning clockwise you see Ailsa Craig, a conical volcanic plug, rising abruptly from the sea, and in clear weather the coast of Ireland. Then comes Kintyre, with Arran in front. To the right of the soaring Goatfell, but farther away, you may see the Paps of Jura. To the right of Arran you meet Kintyre again, and in very clear weather you may see Ben More on distant Mull. On the shores of the Firth of Clyde below you stand Troon, Irvine and Saltcoats/Ardrossan. Next come the Heights of Renfrewshire,

	Landmark	Distance		Height	
		Km	miles	m	ft
1	Brown Carrick Hills (3 communications masts)	18	11	85	279
2	Ayr Harbour	10	6	0	0
	Ailsa Craig to right (Antrim Hills behind)	49	30	338	1109
3	Sanda (off southern tip of Kintyre)	73	45	123	404
4	Pladda (off southern tip of Arran)	39	24	20	66
5	Holy Island, Arran (Lady Isle, Troon, in front)	34	21	314	1030
6	Troon Harbour	6?	4	0	0
7	Goat Fell, Arran	43	27	874	2867
8	Paps of Jura	101	63	785	2575
9	Ardrossan Harbour	22	14	0	0
	Mouth of Loch Fyne	57	35	0	0
10	Ben More, Mull	136	85	967	3173
11	Hill of Stake, Heights of Renfrewshire	36	2	522	1713
12	Crosshouse Hospital	9	6	11	36
	Ben Lomond	74	46	974	3200
13	Earl's Seat, Campsie Fells (Kilmarnock in front)	57	35	578	1896
14	TV mast above Darvel	16	10	351	1152
15	Tinto Hill	55	34	711	2333
16	Hagshaw Hill (wind farm)	39	24	465	1526
17	Mauchline Church tower	9	6	140	459
18	Green Lowther, near Wanlockhead	52	32	732	2402
19	Tarbolton Church tower	3	2	100	328
20	Windy Standard (wind farm)	36	22	698	2290
21	Corserine, Rhinns of Kells	43	27	814	2671
22	Merrick (highest point in mainland S. Scotland)	44	27	843	2766

peaking in the Hill of Stake. Almost due north the rectangular white building, quite close, is Crosshouse Hospital near Kilmarnock. In line with it, the shouldered outline of Ben Lomond is often visible. To its right is Earl's Seat, the highest of the Campsie Fells. The television mast above Darvel is prominent. The next distant peak is Tinto Hill, beyond the M74, followed by Hagshaw Hill with its windfarm. Then come Broad Law, and the twin peaks of Green Lowther and Lowther Hill above Sanquhar. In line, much nearer, is the tower of Mauchline Parish Church. The chipboard factory near Auchinleck is marked by its plume of steam; the headgear of the late Barony colliery is to its right. Next Windy Standard, in the Carsphairn Forest, is distinguished by its windfarm. Corserine in the Rhinns of Kells follow s, then Merrick in the Awful Hand range, amongst several slightly lower peaks. Last comes the Brown Carrick Hill, overlooking Ayr, with its three telecommunication masts.

APPENDIX 2

Prestwick Airport and Scottish Aviation Ltd.

Lord Douglas Douglas-Hamilton, Marquis of Clydesdale (later Duke of Hamilton), and David Fowler McIntyre, both officers in the RAF, made history in 1933 by being the first men to fly over Mount Everest. This achievement may have inspired them to go on to found Scottish Aviation Ltd (SAL) at Prestwick in 1935, their aim being to establish the aviation industry in Scotland. Initially a flying school to train pilots for the RAF was founded. This expanded over the next five years and the requirement to maintain its training aircraft enabled the company to establish a workforce skilled in aircraft engineering. Increased factory space was needed and a solution was found in the purchase of the Palace of Engineering building situated in Bellahouston Park, Glasgow, where it had been part of the 1938 Empire Exhibition. In 1940 it was re-assembled at Monkton, where it still dominates the site.

The Palace of Engineering

McIntyre had ambitious plans for SAL, and during the war the factory became heavily involved in the overhaul and repair of aircraft. After the War the company converted Liberators and Dakotas for airline use. When this work dried up the company manufactured lightweight bus bodies and tractor cabs until the opportunity arose to manufacture its own aircraft, the Prestwick Pioneer, for the short-take-off-and-landing communications rôle. It proved successful and a larger twin-engined version, the Twin Pioneer, followed in 1955. A major setback occurred in December 1957 when David McIntyre and two others were killed when their Twin Pioneer crashed during a sales trip to Libya.

The company continued and found a variety of work including the manufacture and repair of Merlin and Griffon engines, making parts for Hercules aircraft, and an order from Handley Page in 1966 to build the wings for Jetstream turbo-prop airliners, until that company closed in 1969. Another company, Beagle Aircraft, went into receivership in 1970 and SAL secured the rights to build its Bulldog training aircraft, for which there was a substantial outstanding order with the Royal Swedish Air Force. Then in 1972 the Ministry of Defence placed an order for 26 Jetstream communications aircraft, which gave the company the opportunity to introduce a new civil version, the first of which flew in 1978, the year that SAL was nationalised to become part of British Aerospace. The Jetstream proved a great success and more than 300 were sold, mainly in the USA. The company went on to design and manufacture the larger 30-seat Jetstream 41 until the market was lost to the up-and-coming commuter jets. For a number of years, as well as aircraft manufacture, British Aerospace returned to its original intention and operated a training school for pilots at Adamton House (see p.43 and p.53). Today the company is part of BAE Systems and, although no longer making its own aircraft, still employs around 1500 people making major aircraft parts for Airbus, Boeing and others.

INDEX

FURTHER READING

Berry, Peter, *Airfield Focus 42: Prestwick* [Peterborough, 2000]

Brash, Ronald, *The Tramways of Ayr*

Ewart, Jim, *Prestwick Airport Golden Jubilee 1935-1985* [Paisley, 1985]

Fullarton, John (editor), *Records of the Burgh of Prestwick 1470-1782* [Edinburgh, 1834]

Hancock, David, *Citizens of the World* [Cambridge 1995]

Hewat, Kirkwood, *A Little Scottish World* [revised edition, 1908]

Jeffrey, Andrew, *This Time of Crisis: Glasgow, the West of Scotland and the North Western Approaches in the Second World War* [Edinburgh, 1993]

Martin, David, *Auchincruive* [Edinburgh, 1994]

Robertson, Alan, *Lion Rampant and Winged* [Barassie, 1986]

Shaw, James E., *Prestwick Golf Club: A History and Some Records* [Glasgow, 1938]

Smail, David C., *Prestwick Golf Club: Birthplace of the Open* [Prestwick, 1989]

Smith, David J., *Action Stations 7: Military Airfields of Scotland, the North-East and Northern Ireland* [Cambridge, 1983]

Galbraith, William, *Prestwick St Nicholas Golf Club* [Prestwick, 1950]

Steven, Helen J., *Guide to Prestwick and Vicinity* [Paisley, 1897]

Strawhorn, John, *The History of Prestwick* [Edinburgh, 1994]

Whatley, Christopher A., *The Scottish Salt Industry 1570-1850* [Aberdeen, 1987]

NOTES

NOTES

NOTES

NOTES

PUBLICATIONS OF THE AYRSHIRE ARCHÆOLOGICAL AND NATURAL HISTORY SOCIETY

Available from the Publications Distribution Manager,
Ronald Brash MA, 10 Robsland Avenue, Ayr KA7 2RW

Digging Up Old Ayr (Lindsay)	£1.00
George Lokert of Ayr (Broadie)	£1.25
A Scottish Renaissance Household (MacKenzie)	£3.00
Plant Life in Ayrshire (Kirkwood & Foulds)	£4.20
The Barony of Alloway (Hendry)	£3.60
Robert Adam in Ayrshire (Sanderson)	£3.60
The Cumnock Pottery (Quail)	£5.00
Tolls and Tacksmen (McClure)	£3.60
Smuggling and the Ayrshire Economic Boom (Cullen)	£4.00
The Port of Ayr, 1727-1780 (Graham)	£4.20
John Smith of Dalry, Part 1, Geology (ed. Reid)	£6.00
John Smith of Dalry, Part 2, Archaeology and Natural History (ed. Reid)	£7.20
Mauchline Memories of Robert Burns (ed. Strawhorn)	£3.50
Antiquities of Ayrshire (Grose, ed. Strawhorn)	£4.20
Cessnock: an Ayrshire Estate in the Age of Improvement (Mair)	£4.50
Robert Reid Cunninghame of Seabank House (Graham)	£3.60
Historic Ayr; A Guide for Visitors (2nd edition)	£2.50
A Community Rent Asunder: the Newmilns Laceweavers' Strike of 1897 (Mair)	£3.50
The Rise and Fall of Mining Communities in Central Ayrshire (Wark)	£3.00
The Last Miller: The Cornmills of Ayrshire (ed. Wilson)	£6.00
Historic Alloway: Village and Countryside	£2.00
The Street Names of Ayr (Close)	£5.00
Servants in Ayrshire, 1750-1914 (Aitchison)	£5.00
Ayrshire in the Age of Improvement (ed. McClure)	£6.00
Armstrongs' map of Ayrshire, 1775 (6 sheets)	£12.00